Divine
Choreography

Other Books by the Author

Dancing for Him

Dance, Dance, Dance!

Team Terrificus

Dancers' Devotional Calendar

Processionals, Props, & Pageantry

Dance in the Church, What's the Pointe?

Creative Worship

Prophetic Dance

Divine Choreography

Divine Inspirations Choreography Technique

Lynn M. Hayden

Dancing for Him Ministries
Kingston, Massachusetts

SECOND EDITION 2005
Copyright © 2001, Lynn M. Hayden
Dancing For Him Ministries, Inc.
ISBN-10: 0-9771925-1-2
ISBN-13: 978-0-9771925-1-9

Illustrations: Joan B. Machinchick
Lake Claire Design Studio, Annapolis, Maryland
Cover and Book design: Jessica Mitchem
Book Production: SPS Publications, Eustis, Florida
www.spsbooks.com

All rights are reserved. This book is protected under the copyright laws of the United States of America. This book may not be reprinted or copied for commercial gain or profit. The use of short quotations or occasional page copying for personal or group study is permitted and encouraged. No permission is necessary.

Dedication

To my loving, supportive husband, Tom, without whose encouragement, I could not have achieved the numerous attained successes. He has pushed me, pulled me and stretched me beyond where I ever thought I could go. However, if he had not, I don't know where or if I would have gone. To him I owe a debt of gratitude for all the hours he spent driving me to appointments, setting up my tables, bringing me water and consoling me when I thought I wasn't good enough. He's been there for me in the good times and the rough, in the fun times and the sad, during sickness and in health. He's not only been a great husband, but my friend.

Divine Inspirations

Divine ~ "Relating to, or proceeding directly from God (divine love); directed to a deity (divine worship); supremely good; Superb; Heavenly, Godlike."[4]

Inspiration ~ "A divine influence or action on a person believed to qualify him or her to receive and communicate sacred revelation; The action or power of moving the intellect or emotions; The act of influencing or suggesting opinions."[4]

Choreography Technique

Choreography ~ "The art of symbolically representing dancing; The composition and arrangement of dances especially for ballet; A composition created by this art."[4]

Technique ~ "The manner in which technical details are treated (as by a writer) or basic physical movements are used (as by a dancer); ability to treat such details or use such movements (good dance technique); A body of technical methods (as in a craft or in scientific research); A method of accomplishing a desired aim."[4]

Divine Choreography

Introduction 11
Chapter 1 *Where Do I Start?* 15
Chapter 2 *What's Next?* 21
Chapter 3 *Elements of Design* 29
Chapter 4 *Valuable Staging* 41
Chapter 5 *Dance Development* 51
Chapter 6 *Fantastic Finale!* 61
Conclusion 67
Appendix A *Basic Do's & Don'ts* 69
Appendix B *Creative Activations* 73
Index 82
Bibliography 84
Mission Statement 85

Divine Choreography

Introduction

"Flesh gives birth to flesh, but the Spirit gives birth to spirit." (John 3:6)

"Intellectual conclusions, derived from movement expression take time to be analyzed. However, the spirit of a man can already receive ministry before the mind has time to figure out what happened. *Divine inspirations* allow us to tangibly experience God's presence. Often, when viewers observe *choreography technique*, that is truly inspired of the Lord, they may not understand or know what to believe, but they will have already been touched and experienced God's love. **Divine choreography** that is born of the Spirit will give birth to spirit; thereby moving the heart and charming the soul."

The Lord has placed in my heart the mandate to produce information that will help others focus on the visions that He gives and afford the worshipper techniques with which to bring them to completion. Although some of the concepts are a little complicated, no one expects you to absorb and use all of them right away. Just being aware of the different techniques will help. After pouring through the text, some of the concepts will remain in your mind, while others will come back to your remembrance during the preparation process. Don't get bogged down with trying to memorize all the techniques or analyses of movement. Maybe take one concept a week and incorporate it into your dance team practice times (using appendix B). What ever you do, don't get discouraged if you don't use or understand all the concepts. What ever offering you bring to the Lord (if it is presented with a humble and submissive worshippers' heart) will be a sweet smelling savor to our Lord. The idea behind being aware of dance composition concepts is not to make you feel like you can't present a dance if you don't use them.

It is to enhance your movement vocabulary and knowledge, so when and if you do use them, the dances will become more enjoyable.

I've had the privilege of being able to choreograph dances in very small spaces and in very large spaces. I've danced in front of an audience of one as well as a crowd of ten thousand and everything in between. In most of the scenarios, I was able to use one concept or another. Often, it wasn't even until after the Lord had given me the dance that I discovered or remembered that I was using one of the techniques, or during the process of choreography, did He bring it back to mind. One time I was just showing one person a dance that I had been working on with which I wasn't particularly impressed. However, it moved her to tears.

Sometimes, depending on the size of the stage or facility, I have to do some instant 're-choreographing'. When I first did a solo to "I Will Worship," I did it in a fairly large church of about three hundred or so. I had plenty of room to express the full message of the dance and it was well received.

The next church that asked me to do that solo was located in a very small storefront. I had just completed a weekend worship dance workshop at one church, and one of the participants asked me to come to their church (across town) on Sunday evening, to do a dance. I had no idea what size the church was or how its seats were arranged or anything. They did mention that it was a storefront church, though. When I arrived and they showed me my dance space, I prayed quickly for divine re-creation. It was literally a four foot by four foot square with two aisles (one of which was very close to the wall). When I danced, I literally bumped into the wall two times! Nevertheless, the whole church proceeded to flow into continual and intense worship upon completion of the dance.

By contrast, I've also had the exhilarating experience of dancing in front of ten thousand people where running across the front area of the church could wipe somebody out if they weren't in shape.

Then, there was the time that I choreographed a piece for one hundred dancers in a stadium for the Olympics, using fifty of the five-yard worship cloths.

Divine Choreography

The point is that no matter how many people in front of whom you are, or how large the stage space is, are you doing spontaneous or choreographed movements that evoke a response of praise, worship or ministry?

In this book, we will explore this and learn how to choreograph from the entrance and introduction all the way through dance development to the ending and exit. Each chapter is filled with ideas to help anyone make their dance presentations minister most effectively. I trust that this resource will help you accomplish that which the Lord has for you to present and that your divine inspirations along with good choreography techniques make beautiful divine choreography for our King!

1

Where Do I Start?

In The Beginning...
A Communication Form of Spirit Design

In The Beginning...

The best place to start your divine choreography is in the beginning with the book of Genesis. We see here that God created (Gen. 1:1). This means that our God is creative. The word *create*, that is mentioned in the first sentence of the Bible, comes from the root word bara' which means: "to form or fashion, to produce, to create."[1] The Word Wealth (from the Spirit Filled Life Bible) states: "Originally this verb carried the idea of carving or cutting out, and that concept is still expressed by the intensive verbal form in Josh. 17:18, referring to cutting down trees to clear out the land. This suggests that creating is similar to sculpturing. Thus bara' is a fitting word to describe both creating by *bringing into existence and creating by fashioning existing matter into something new,* as God did in creating man out of dust from the ground. God is always the subject of the verb bara' in its standard form: creating is therefore a divine capacity."[2]

Let us take this revelation about the word create, combine it with some of the definitions of divine inspirations and choreography techniques, then we will have a formula for successful dance ministry. Since creating is a divine capacity that brings into existence something from nothing and fashions existing matter into something new, then a divine inspiration that proceeds directly from God can be received and communicated as sacred revelation which can produce power that moves the intellect or emotions. Hence, divine inspirations. Going a little deeper, we can combine that with the art of symbolically representing dance with an understanding of how physical movements are used and the ability to use such movements, thereby choreography technique.

In other words, our God is a creative God who not only formed and fashioned things from nothing but also took existing things and made something new. Since the act of creating is a divine capacity, then the divine inspirations that we receive from God give us the creative ability to communicate this revelation to others. This may be done through dance movement with the purpose and intent to touch someone's heart, thereby initiating a regeneration of the soul. We, as born again believers, house the living God in our earthly temples. Therefore, since He is the creator, how much more are we divinely able to communicate His heart through creative movements? Not only that, but we, like our indwelling creator, can create dances from absolutely nothing (through divine inspiration) and we are able to create something brand new from movement ideas and techniques that are already available and proven.

The key, then, to divine inspirations within our choreography, is our personal relationship with our Lord, from whom all blessings (and inspiration) flow... It is in the beginning...the onset of creativity and symbiotic relationship from where we get our start; and here that our communication form (creative choreography) can express the Holy Spirit's design for this day and hour.

A Communication Form of Spirit Design

This synergistic relationship can accomplish several things. The Spirit of the Lord is truly quite an artist. Take a look around at nature's beauty: multitudes of colorful flowers; a dense forest of trees in the autumn season; or a peaceful lake, with mountains in the background, just to name a few. His communication form

Divine Choreography

is like design or art. If we really look, we can notice artistic design in just about everything. How about the way your home is decorated (not just a painting on the wall)? Are there many different shapes, heights, and dimensions of the furniture? What about the straight lines in space fashioned by windows or walls? Contrast those with the soft curved nature of pillows and throws. Add to those different shaped nick-knacks then pepper that with dried flower arrangements. This design recipe, within one room or a whole house creates messages and feelings of comfort, peace, joy, and interest. Certainly, there are many ways to express or communicate what the Spirit is saying. There is verbal communication, such as preaching; dramatic form, as through mime, dramas, and musicals; among others, of course, there is the specific form of dance accompanied by music. Herein lies the crux of our discussion.

Music, after all, is usually where the creative process begins. I know when I hear a certain song that witnesses with my spirit, it seems as though the inspiration wheels begin to churn. This is where I always start. Sometimes, I try to find a song that is appropriate for a certain occasion (wedding, communion, Easter, Christmas, Etc.). This process is slightly onerous because it is not a natural flow of inspiration. However, once I find this type of song, then I listen to it repeatedly and begin to pray. I ask the Lord to show me an interpretation. I usually take the opportunity during car travel to give the song incessant audition. I listen to it over, and over again until I get something. Usually, a dance will come to me like a photograph is developed. First, I see a vague outline (almost blurry figures, if you will), like the picture seen on photographic paper that is dipped into its first developing solution. Later, after listening and praying some more, the design becomes a little clearer, like the paper being dipped into its second solution tray. Finally, I get a complete vision with many parts for different people, with props (sometimes), and even some of the specific movements (getting the movements at this stage, however, takes a little practice and familiarity with dance and its vocabulary). Do not feel like you have to see movements at this stage, because the rest of this book is designed to help you with choreography techniques and ideas. This final 'vision' stage is like the final image seen on the photographic paper as it sits in the 'fixer' or finishing solution. Once I get to this stage (usually after a long car trip to the city), I experiment with some steps and movements at home. I will explain this process more specifically, later.

Sometimes, people will give me certain songs for certain events for which they want me to choreograph something. To me, this is the most difficult type of assignment, because I have to catch on to someone else's vision. This is not to say that it cannot be done, as it most certainly can and is often anointed. I'm just saying that it is a little less personally inspirational. One time I was given a song for which I agreed to choreograph and coordinate a fairly large group. I listened to that song more then any other that I can recall and it took me the longest time to get any ideas. Finally, when I would get something and try it out on the dancers, I found that it didn't really work like I had seen and I had to change it. I changed this dance so many times that it began to become frustrating. I began to wonder if I should have accepted the assignment. Back to prayer, I went and finally, it worked together for our good. If you get an assignment like this, don't give up (unless you know that it is not meant to be done) and continue to pray and maybe even fast (as the Lord directs). Nevertheless, I still followed the same process of design acquisition (lots of prayer and repetitious listening to the song).

My absolute favorite type of choreography comes from the song where the inspiration is almost instant. One time, I was driving in the van, listening to Christian radio. Most of the music and chatter was not even noticeable until I heard this one particular song. It seemed to jump out of the radio at me and say: "make this a dance"! Instantly, as the song was playing, I saw almost the entire 'fixer' stage dance. When I got to the grocery store, I pulled in the parking lot and continued listening to the rest of the song, until its completion. There was tremendous witness to the vision's validity. We worked, easily on the dance, in few practices and it was very anointed and well received. Occurrences like this happen periodically, and it is so wonderful when it does. Most of the time, though, the type of

Divine Choreography

songs I do, fall in between this and the first type mentioned. When you find a song, think about what type it is and its appropriate application for the given occasion. Songs that speak *to* God, reach the throne room with our praise, worship, and adoration. The songs that talk *about* God, can reach the heart of man through presentations, representing the Word of God. Finally, songs that come *from* God to the recipient can express the heart of the Father (prophetically). Each of these types of songs can be a communication form of Spirit design that, in conjunction with divine inspirations facilitate the creation of divine choreography.

What's Next?

Assimilation of Spirit Design Demonstrated Through Human Vessels
Solo or Group
Grand Entrances & Introductions

Assimilation of Spirit Design Demonstrated Through Human Vessels

In the first chapter, we covered some of the Spiritual aspects of our divine inspirations. The remaining chapters cover the implementation of practical aspects of choreography and techniques that make your presentations minister most effectively. Assuming you already have an understanding of the importance of prayer, fasting and listening to the music prior to putting the steps together, then what comes next is the assimilation of your Spirit design demonstrated through human vessels. So, at this point, choreography techniques play a large role.

When watching dance presentations, think about how you are affected by some more then others. Why do you think this is so? The main reason, of course, is the anointing. However, aside from that (since we will be talking about technique in this section) do you find your mind wandering or wishing it were more interesting? Do you only love the dance because you love the people in it, or did it really minister to your heart? The idea behind good choreography is to capture someone's heart before his or her mind has had time to comprehend. In other words, if a dance piece is very interesting and has a lot of variety, it will, more then likely, hold the audience's attention longer and thereby minister more effectively. Conversely, if a piece has little variation, the audience may tend to be disinterested. Therefore, it may not have a chance to penetrate their hearts. I do not speak out of condemnation, but experience.

One time, I was asked if my team or I had a dance ready for presentation. The church needed a special for that particular Sunday service (which happened to be the next day). I had been working on a solo at home, but it was only at the very early stages of development. I stepped out in faith (or took a risk) and said: "sure, I'll do something." At the time, I wasn't really well versed in spontaneity, but I basically 'wung it' anyway. I hadn't taken into consideration that the song was very long (an issue I will discuss later) and I quickly ran out of interesting things to do. So, I began repeating myself. I could literally *feel* that I had lost the audience. Basically, they were getting bored. They applauded, I believe, out of love and obligation. I don't believe the song really ministered. It was more like the "half-time" half-entertainment. I learned my lessons: first, to pray before obligating; second, use good choreography techniques to keep the audience's attention; and finally, use a shorter song for a solo.

Throughout the remainder of the book, we will discuss many different techniques so that when put into practice; your presentation pieces will shine wonderfully. In this particular chapter, we will cover some foundational topics for a good beginning.

Solo or Group

When assimilating your Spirit design, one of the first decisions to be made is how many people should be in your demonstrative piece. So many times, in the prayerful, thought

Divine Choreography

processes, I would be caught up in the anointing of the song and start out with one person in my mind, then end up with practically a stadium sized production. There has to be a happy medium, particularly if you only have four or five willing participants. Sometimes, this boundary is an automatic guide. The key, again, is what the Lord is saying to you about the dance (either by impression, voice, or vision). In our vast human creativity, we can tend to accelerate into ambition, leaving anointing behind. We want to avoid this at all costs.

If you only have four dedicated team members, don't let that stop your vision, however, should it grow to what seems a disproportionate size. Many times, if you see flag, banner, cloth or prop incorporation, you can recruit temporary worshippers, with little or no experience, to fill those slots. They can then be released to the pews upon piece completion and presentation. I have done this many times successfully and the participants were very satisfied that they were able to be a part. They were also relieved at the release of further obligation. On the other hand, this temporary recruitment often turned into permanent placement of a new dance team member or two, who may have just wanted to initially 'get their feet wet'.

One good indicator (of whether to do a solo or a group dance) is the length of the song. If you have a very long song (seven minutes or more), it is usually best to have several, people and props. The mere fact that you have many people moving creates interest. When you have numbers of people doing a wide variety of movements and using a lot of space, this in and of itself creates great appeal. Therefore, when there is a long piece of music, there is much more that can be done within its confines, to maintain the curiosity and concentration of your audience. Hence, there is potential ministry. Unless you are highly skilled or extremely anointed when attempting that same long song as a solo, it becomes increasingly more difficult to maintain high interest and evoke ministerial response.

Another very important tip about doing a group dance (particularly if it is large) is to keep the unison movements very simple. Cut off all the extra, unnecessary movement. For example: if you wanted everyone, all at the same time, to do some kind of windmill or backstroke type of arm movements, everyone would have their own version. It would be much better to have everyone simply hold the arms up in a diagonal fashion and change their position only once or twice. This has a much more clean look. It is also a good idea to keep the whole dance in general, fairly simple, again because many people create complexity. Too much complication sometimes creates confusion (particularly if there is no coherence within the piece).

In a smaller group dance (two to four people), be careful not to make a solo with more people. This is where the whole group does almost all the same things all the same way, all the same direction with no variation. What this is essentially is a solo done with more people. If this were the case, you could just eliminate the other three dancers and simply do a solo. The idea though is to add lots of variety. Later, we will look at numerous different kinds of variations that can be incorporated into your dances.

When doing a solo, it is best to have a short song (about three to four minutes), if possible. It is much better to have the audience wanting more then to have them wishing there was no more. Unlike the large group dance, a solo has much more freedom to be complex and should be. There should be abundant variety of movement since there is only one person expressing the entire idea or message of the song. A specific idea should be established, developed, and repeated throughout the piece in varying forms. Variety is great, but enough repetition should be there to confirm the image or idea that is being portrayed. In other words, try to maintain a certain theme with the movements. Be careful not to do dances with *so many* different types of movements (albeit extremely creative), that there is no repetition of any one move, hence any continuity or theme understanding.

Also, in a solo, one person has the entire stage, front area of the church, and the aisles (possibly) to fill, making variety a little more difficult. I suppose it depends on how you view things, though. The space availability could be used to your advantage exactly for the variety you need. When I do a solo,

Divine Choreography

I like to go out to the audience and make direct contact with them. Of course, the song must lend itself that way. It would be quite inappropriate to reach to someone in the audience if the song were saying: "I lift up my eyes to the hills." On the other hand, if the lyrics say: "Let Me comfort your soul beside My still waters," then going out and motioning to an individual in the audience would be very appropriate. Once you've come to a conclusion, whether to do a solo or a dance with more then one person, then you are ready to begin with the entrance and introduction.

Grand Entrances and Introductions

Entrances (or entering the viewing area) need not necessarily be grand. In fact, most songs begin somewhat softly or quietly, and then build in complexity and strength. The dance should generally follow suit. Entering from the back of the auditorium and moving toward the front stage area of the church is good. However, be mindful that the majority of the audience is not aware or cannot see what is going on during an entrance of this type. They may miss some of the message of the dance. Although this is primarily done during traditional processional type dances, it may apply to other forms as well. As I mentioned in the Processional book, it is a good idea (if you feel that the dance should begin from the back of the sanctuary) to have some type of activity going on in the front or on the stage. For example: a large banner could travel across the front, or a dancer could begin on stage; or two flag bearers could cross one another and circle around each other before finding their place. These types of things would very well hold the audience's attention while the remaining dancers make their way down the aisle.

Another kind of entrance is simply making a formation and walking to your place on the stage or floor before the music begins. This should be treated with as much reverential consideration as the dance itself. Of course, it all depends on where your "off stage" is. If your dance is supposed to begin with the music after you are on the stage, and the only way you can get to the stage is from the back of the church, then I would recommend walking very uniformly down the aisle with little or no extraneous movements or nervous chatter. Once you get to the front, place yourselves in the most organized fashion possible. In other words, if you have, say four dancers that are to begin on the stage with two in the front and two in the back, then have the two back line dancers enter the stage first and the front line enter last. Be mindful of what direction they all turn around to face the front (all to the right or all to the left). This may seem like a minor detail, but it will improve your overall presentation. Certainly, you can be creative with your entrances. For instance: if you have six people in the dance, you could have two enter from one side, two enter from the other side, and two come from the center (again, being mindful of your uniformity and turn direction, once in place). The possibilities for entrance are endless with one thread of consistency and that is reverential uniformity and organized placement.

If you are to enter with the music, this warrants a discussion about musical introductions. In keeping with the chapter title: "What's Next?," sequentially, it is typically the introduction of the song. The introduction is usually eight, sixteen, thirty-two, or sixty-four counts of music (without words). There are of course exceptions to the rule, but generally speaking, this is usually the case. Depending on the music and the number of people in the dance, you could easily enter during the introduction, from any number of locations. This is usually less awkward then placement before the music. Again, this depends on the song.

If you do place yourself or others before the music begins (during a silent entrance), try not to just stand there during the musical introduction (in anticipation of the words). It will seem like the longest sixty-four counts in history that your audience will experience as well. It is a good idea to do some movement, even if it is very minimal. Another point that I will just interject here, and kind along the same lines, is to not have periods in the song where the audience is left to interpret the music for themselves. Let me explain. If you were doing a solo and the song said something like: "Angels we have heard on high, sweetly singing over the plane and the mountains in reply, echoing their joyous strain," don't stand motionless in the middle of the stage,

Divine Choreography

letting the audience imagine angels over head on one side and mountains singing on the other. Interpret!

Also, it is not necessary to give away the whole idea of the song in the beginning. Develop the song slowly by letting the story evolve. Keep your introductions simple. Simplicity can be the introduction of one dancer or banner before the others appear, or it could be simplicity of the movement of several dancers.

If you seem somewhat overwhelmed by your overall vision of the dance, begin working on the introduction. Start with getting movement or steps for the first four beats of music. It may be as uncomplicated as raising your arm up two counts and bringing it down two counts. Go back and review your first four counts and then progress on to the next four counts. Once you've accomplished movements to your liking, review the first four AND the second four. Then go on to the next four or eight counts and go back from the beginning to there. Repeat this process until you feel very comfortable and get familiar with the introduction. Remember, you will have prayed about and gotten some kind of vision or impression for the dance, so the movements that you do should reflect that idea in some manner. Start by doing what comes out naturally and build from there.

Once you've prayed through the assimilation of the Spirit's design; decided whether it is to be a solo or group dance; mastered the entrance and introduction; then you should be ready to incorporate more detailed choreography techniques, using elements of design.

3
Elements of Design

Motif
Symmetry
Copy, Complement & Contrast

Motif

Elements of design are simply parts, ideas, or pieces that comprise the whole. They are also concepts of choreography or composition that can and should be used to help shape and mold the dance. They are techniques that make a dance composition become more interesting and come alive. One element of design is a *motif* (moteef). "Motif is a movement or movement phrase that not only is the first part of or starting point of a composition; but that which has been selected, evaluated, refined and the initial motivating force for the rest of the dance."[3] Basically, it is the initial theme and common thread of movement throughout the dance. In John 3:3, Jesus answered and said to him, "Most assuredly, I say to you, unless one is born again, he cannot see the kingdom of God."[2] Like a motif is the starting point and theme of a dance, being born again or letting Jesus Christ be Lord of our entire life is the starting point of our life's composition. We will be refined into His image if He remains our motivating force throughout our life.

Examples of motifs are practically endless. However, for

clarity's sake I will explain some basics, first. These words, movements, and movement phrases should give you enough creative stimulation to last a long time. In the explanation process, we are going to use Laban's Analysis of Movement. This is a basic overview of various types of movement. It is broken down into four parts:

Actions of the Body	Qualities of Movement
Spatial Environment	Relating to objects or people

Within each of these categories, there are a number of movement types that can be incorporated with a motif to create an interesting dance. By simply reading the list of words, your mind will already be open and begin to visually see all kinds of varieties of basic movements. For example:

1. **"Actions of the Body**
   Jump
   Gesture
   Turn
   Travel
   Twist
   Stretch
   Bend
   Transference of Weight – Stepping
   Stillness – Balance

2. **Qualities of Movement – Dynamics**
   Flow – Bound (Stoppable)
   Flow – Free (On Going)
   Weight – Relaxed
   Weight – Light
   Weight – Firm
   Time – Slow
   Time – Sustained
   Time – Sudden, Quick

3. **Spatial Environment**
   Size of Movement (Large, Medium, or Small)
   Size of Space (Large, Medium, or Small)

Divine Choreography

      Extension in Space
      Levels (Low, Medium, and High)
      Shape in Space (Curved or Straight
      Pathways (Floor Patterns)
      Pathways (Air Patterns)
      Pathways (Curved or Straight)
      Directions in Space (Depth, Width, Height)
      Directions in Space (Planes)
      Directions in Space (Diagonals)

4. **Relationship**
      Numerical Variation – Succession
      Group Shape
      Inter-Group (Relating to One Another)
      Spatial Relationship (Over, Under, or Around)
      Duets
            Copying - Mirroring
            Leading – Following
            Unison – Cannon
            Meeting – Parting
            Question – Answer"[3]

    Before moving on to the specific motif examples, I'd like to explain what some of these terms mean and how they may be applied. Some of them are quite obvious and don't need explanation. However, for instance, in the qualities of movement, you'll notice several dynamics, including: time, weight, and flow. Dynamics are essential for attention-grabbing dances. They are simply movements with a varying intensity range like unto the difference between the sharpness of a sewing needle to the silkiness of chocolate moose. Any and all of these dynamics may be used individually or together. Some of them are opposites from one another and would create wonderful variety if used that way. For example: if you were to use allegro (fast) music and combine it with sharp, accurate movements or even fast spins, it would generate stimulating excitement.
    On the other hand, if there was moderato (moderate tempo) or adagio (slow tempo) type music and with it, you demonstrated smooth even rounded type movements, it would create an

atmosphere of peace with soothing results. More specifically, if you were to do movement that was very free flowing, on going or continuous, then suddenly stopped the flow (bound-stoppable) by coming to a screeching halt, it would create an element of surprise. This type of contrast creates momentary fascination. If you first went from a firm stance (standing motionless like a solid wall) then suddenly went into movements that made you appear very light (like a hot air balloon) and finally went into a "Raggedy Ann" doll-type mode, this dynamic weight change would offer much variety. Be mindful, however, not to repeat any one dynamic too often, because it would loose its edge or appeal. The idea is to use them to create interest and variety.

Likewise, with regard to relationship, group shapes can be very interesting when incorporated into your choreography. Different types of numerical variations or movements in succession are quite exciting to watch. This is where, let's say, the group is in a vertical line one behind the other and the front person does a movement and then on every beat of music, the others behind that one does the same or similar movements one at a time in succession. We will talk more about the variations of this later in the Cannon section.

I must comment on the duets portion. Those few words in that list are vital to a good duet. By the way, it is wise not to do a duet with all the same movements facing front, as that becomes too flat and could be dull. Conversely, these movement suggestions are marvelously worthy of note. Meeting and parting is particularly good. It is the type of movement that is quite prevalent in a ballet pas de deux (dance of two). This is usually where the male and female dancers play kind of a chase and catch game with one another. They will come together for a sustained moment and then part to other parts of the stage.

One caution when doing this type of movement is to avoid "split screen." In other words, if you do come together in the middle and split apart, try not to go to opposite sides of the stage from one another and stay there. The audience then has to watch one side of the stage or the other. It can be frustrating for them because they will want to watch both. It would be better to briefly visit the opposite sides and then quickly come

Divine Choreography

together again perhaps in another part of the stage with a different kind of shape or movement.

Question and answer is also another relationship concept that is very appealing for incorporation. This is where one dancer would do a movement or movement phrase indicative of the music. The second dancer would do a different movement, kind of in response to the first's. Hence, question and answer. This type of movement lends itself well to music that has an echo effect.

Now that we have a basic understanding about the analysis of movement, we can proceed on to a more specific example of Motif. I would like to go over the motif of *repetition* now and *change* in a later chapter. More specifically, I'll go over some concepts with repetition through development and variation, using the analysis of movement. Let's say that the following would be used during the climax or highlight of the dance.

Action Phrases—Within the following movement phrases, stillness before or after often creates a 'gut' reaction in the audience.

- "Rise
- Travel
- Close (movements going into inward, into yourself)
- Fall
- Open (wide, large, spread out type movements)
- Gesture leading into turn
- Travel into a balance
- Tip into transference of weight
- Travel and leap"[3]

Can you see how just the mention of these types of movement phrases could evoke a good response, especially if done with complete stillness or suspension before or after?

Quality Phrases—Let's try the same concept with quality phrases only think of sudden or even subtle change of qualities or a build up in force or time or both.

- "From firm tension, gradually loosen tension to become light
- Move quickly and lightly
- Release all tension and collapse

- Travel quickly and with free flow to end in sudden and firm stillness
- Move slowly with change in tensions
- Move quickly alternating between firm and light qualities
- Spin, accelerating and decelerating to end in a firm body shape"[3]

When these types of movements are incorporated into a dance with purpose and motivation, they can produce an emotional response within the viewer.

Spatial Phrases—Moving on within the analysis of movement, spatial phrases relate to change in the amount of space that is used or the focus in space and even the stage placement. With this in mind, let's examine some examples.

- "Move with a constantly changing focus
- Change focus and then move (repeat this three times)
- Start with very small movements and increase in size to very large
- Intersperse large and small movements
- Move slightly right and then left
- Move in a series of curves to end center front"[3]

The possibilities are endless. These can be done with one or more people and in various directions. These types of movements done during the highlight of the dance will surely have an instant reaction in the captivated audience.

Relationship Phrases—Finally, we will cover variation or contrast in group relationships. This is simply the addition or subtraction in the number of people moving in the stage space, and the variation in how they relate to one another.

- Start in a closed circle or 'clump' and suddenly become scattered and unrelated or go from being scattered and unrelated (all over the stage) to drawing close together in a related formation.
- Move from a closed (shoulder to shoulder) line to a spread out line
- Move from a single row to two, three, or four rows
- Have everyone who is spread out in various places hold,

Divine Choreography

while #1 moves toward #2, then #'s 1&2 move to #3, then all three move to #4

Think of relationships like a kaleidoscope. All the elements or multicolored pieces of glass, are used over and over again in a myriad of shapes, formations and designs. Nevertheless, they always relate to one another in some fashion. As the tube turns, the same elements continually change to form something entirely new and different. These types of changes and variations could and should be used throughout the dance and don't necessarily have to be reserved for the highlight. They are good movement ideas for any part of the dance to add interest.

Basically, the motif is the motivating force or theme demonstrated throughout the dance. It has the potential for development. The idea, then, is to use these movement phrases in combination with the motif. Each of the movement phrases that are used to express the motif should repeat, using variety. They should be done in different ways, with different people, in different parts of the stage, yet the same type of phrase within the motif. There are several other elements of design that can be incorporated and that will be discussed, but it was essentially important to learn this lengthy foundation. This depth of understanding, comprehension, and utilization could change your dances forever, and done effectively, will produce inspiring works of art and a sweet smelling savor to our Lord.

Symmetry

Symmetry combined with asymmetry and amalgamated with both movement phrases and varying pathways on the floor create vastly different moods and emotions. The definition of symmetry is: "similarity of form or arrangement on either side of a dividing line or plane; correspondence of opposite parts in size, shape, and position; condition of being symmetrical; the whole or the corresponding parts are said to have symmetry; balance or beauty of form or proportion resulting from such correspondence."[4] "For now we see in a mirror, dimly, but then face to face."[2] (I Cor. 13:12) "Ancient mirrors, which were manufactured at Corinth, were made of metal and gave dim reflections, an illustration of our imperfect knowledge during this age. But knowledge will be full and instantaneous in the future state of glory."[2]

There are several forms through which symmetry and asymmetry may be demonstrated. It may be done within the body, itself with one person, or several people doing the same symmetrical pose or movements. It is like a mirror, so if you raise, let's say the right arm up to a diagonal, a symmetrical movement would be to likewise raise the left arm. If a group were doing it, they would all begin by raising the right arm and then the left. The dividing line or plane is down the center of each dancer's body. Symmetry could be expressed by one person or group of people maintaining a certain pose or doing a certain movement on one side of the stage, while another individual or group does a very similar movement on the other side of the dividing line down the center of the stage. It would look almost like a double image.

Symmetrical Design

Say you had three people on the left side of the stage facing the center line and they were all reaching both arms up on a diagonal. They could be on different levels from one another (low, medium, and high). A symmetrical pose would be to have another group of three people on the right side of the stage, facing into the center and holding the same pose. Perhaps there would be a cross, banner, or main character in the center to which everyone would be pointing.

Also, certain pathways on the floor, going in one direction, may be repeated in like fashion on the other side of the stage. This is almost like taking a book with a design freshly printed on one page, and then closing the book so the impression transfer in opposition onto the other page. This could become, for instance, your opposing or symmetrical pathways that could be converted to stage space. For example: one

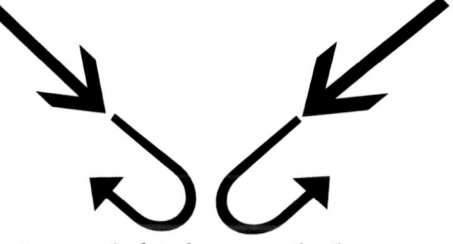

Symmetrical Pathways on the floor

dancer could come from upstage right, move to downstage left, and turn in a clockwise direction and pose. A second dancer could come from upstage left, move to downstage right, do a counterclockwise turn, and pose. Another way to present the same idea is to have the number one dancer or group of dancers do the first type of pathway on the floor space and then, to make good use of the entire stage space, repeat this movement on the other side (instead of using another dancer or group). Be cautious here, though, because if symmetry is done too often, it can become predictable and loose creative spark.

When doing asymmetrical shapes, designs, or pathways on the floor, there is no need to repeat it on the other side. The definition of asymmetrical is basically a lack of symmetry. That is the whole idea behind asymmetry: variation by creating differences instead of sameness. Both symmetrical and asymmetrical designs should be used. Symmetrical movements and poses seem to give a feeling of completeness and satisfaction, which make a good ending for a dance. On the other hand, asymmetrical design adds captivating anticipation. However, the use of both, throughout the dance, adds to the overall visual inspiration.

Copy, Complement & Contrast

Dance is really a visual, motion-filled art form. It is almost like a motion picture, if you will, with many different 'photo frames'. Though it is for the most part, in continuous movement, if the film were to stop, each 'dance frame' should be seen as lovely design. This can be quite satisfying to the audience if the right relationships are in place. These relationships between the various dancers may be enhanced through poses or movements that demonstrate copying, complementing, or contrasting effects. A copy relationship between the dancers is pretty straightforward and easy to understand and visualize. It is simply the exact repetition of a line, design, shape, or pose. One person copies the other one's position or movement exactly.

Copy Relationship

Complementary movement reemphasizes, makes more of, makes bigger, or fills in a movement or visual communication. This is where one person does a particular move or pose and another does something very similar (same type of shape or position) only it has some characteristic that is slightly different. It is used to enhance a movement or pose. For example: one person may be on their knees, facing a diagonal, with their arms curved upwards with the back arm slightly higher then the front and the other person would be behind and a little to the side, perhaps standing with their arms in the same formation. The difference, here is in the levels. This can be done with a larger group as well as two people. Nevertheless, it adds quite a bit of variety.

Complimentary Relationship

Finally, repetitions of contrasting movement lines or shapes hold another type of meaningful image. It is primarily oppositional type movement. Strong, straight, angular type movements with a sharp nature, often suggest force, create excitement, and strengthen the meaning as well as the impression or tone of the dance. However, this, though by itself creates strength, when it is combined with soft rounded type movements, gives new meaning and depth. Soft, curved, rounded movements usually give a feeling of grace and loveliness. These types of movements tend to flow well with (but are not limited to) softer, slower, more

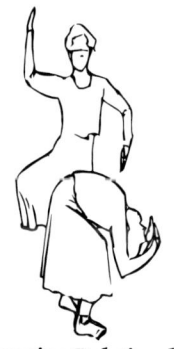

Contrasting Relationship

melodic music. The opposing movement genre, of straight verses curved, may be accomplished with one, two, or many people; during still poses or through movement, using body shapes, pathways on the floor, and pathways in the air.

A simply basic, purely artistic pose-type contrast example might be: one person would stand straight with arms angularly shaped overhead while someone else might pose in front of them contracted over in a ball-like shape.

For an example of something a little more complex, let us envision a movement sequence (within a particular dance), with two opposing groups. Let's say group A (on one side of the stage) were moving in straight-line pathways on the floor, straight angular body shapes, primarily in a tall vertical body positioning (with possibly even an occasional jumping up motion), toward those on the other side of the stage. For contrast, the opposing team (group B) could do soft, melodic movements with curved (bent over) body shapes and curved pathways on the floor, as they gracefully move toward their militant opponent. The anticipation of their coming together is rather gripping, but when these design shapes converge in the center, momentarily, the visual effect is quite good.

Whether simple or complex, with one person or many, using the elements of design such as motif, symmetry, or copy, complement, and contrast, will open new discovery doors for your choreography.

Divine Choreography

4

Valuable Staging

Is This My Better Side?
Stage Placement
Value of Direction of Movement

Is This My Better Side?

If I were to subtitle this section, it would be named: strength of body positioning and alignment. It is very important for the dancer (particularly a soloist) to face the best direction for a particular pose. There are certain strengths and weaknesses that positions hold. For instance, if the dancer or dancers were facing directly front with no angular positioning of the body, this would be the strongest type positioning. In other words, it would have the greatest impact and leave the strongest image or impression. This is certainly not to say that we should remain there or get stuck facing front because we have this understanding. How boring would that be? However, during the majority of the dance, and when there is going to be particular emphasis during a certain part in the dance it could be done facing front for good effect.

Much to many people's surprise, facing directly back carries almost as much weight as facing front. This is a very strong body position for dramatic emphasis. One time, I choreographed a dance, with quite a number of people (as it was part of a conference, so the participants were involved). During one segment, the dancers all ran up on the stage in the center and toward the back (or upstage center, which we will talk about in the next section). When they all got together, in a bunch, shoulder to shoulder facing back, the words of the song said: "mighty, mighty, mighty is the Lord." On the last mighty, they all raised their right fist straight overhead. Then, on Lord, they all turned right and made their fists turn into an 'L' shape (as in sign language) and slowly brought it down in front of them, maintaining a straight arm. The effect of the group facing back, with fists in the air, was surprisingly powerful.

As body positions gradually shift directions to the right or left (from front), they grow increasingly weaker. By the time someone is facing upstage left, let's say, that body positioning loses quite a bit of value. However, that is not to say that this type of directional positioning does not have any merit. It can be used to your advantage. For example: if you had a time during the song where you wanted to feature one dancer, you could have the remaining dancers become almost obscure, or indistinct, by having them all face in a diagonally upstage body position. By the way, an important tip to remember is that the audience's eye is drawn toward that which moves the most. So, in this case, all the attention would be on that solo dancer, while the others seem shrouded.

Alignment

Alignment of the body during certain type of poses or positions plays an important roll. This is a little different then the basic directions that the dancers face for effect. This is in reference to specific body positioning for certain poses. Suppose you wanted to do an arabesque. This is where a dancer stands on one leg and extends the other leg out behind the body, while one arm extends out in front of the body. Then the body tilts forward, slightly to compensate for the leg extension. If this particular pose is done with the hand reaching directly toward the audience and the foot reaching toward the back of the stage,

Divine Choreography

the audience would never capture the beauty of the pose. If the audience were standing off stage, behind the curtains, they would have a great view! Simply turn the pose 90 degrees so that the hand is reaching toward the side of the stage. Then the audience will get the full effect of the view. Think about this with any interesting pose that you do. Try doing it facing different directions and see which is most pleasing to the eye.

I must interject a helpful 'side note' comment here. It is wise to practice an arabesque and other more difficult movements, in the privacy of your home or in a dance class. Practice and improve your skill continually. If you are unable to execute a movement on stage with ease, don't do it. Many times, when people (including myself) try to do this arabesque (or what's known as a penche, which is like it only you lean over further while balancing) or fancy leaps or turns, it ends up getting muddled. So often, people want to do a "tour jete," which is a turn in the air while kicking and switching the legs in the air. When an accomplished dancer does this, it is delightful and lovely. On the other hand, when someone attempts to do it on stage and they really don't have it down well, it can have disastrous results. Knees are bent. Toes are not pointed. Balance is lost. This is not to say that we have to be a member of the New York City Ballet to do worship dance – certainly not! What happens is that when a more difficult movement is not executed with grace, it becomes a little awkward, and then what the audience notices is the mistake instead of the style. For a brief moment in the audience's mind, something goes: "oops!" as they have empathy for the untrained dancer. The result is that the mistakes become a distraction from the overall message of the dance.

It would be much more effective to do a similar type of movement that is scaled way down in the level of difficulty. Do something that kind of looks like that movement where you are easily able to maintain balance and control. I do this myself. During a ballet class, I may be able to beautifully execute a double pirouette (spin on one leg). However, during a ministry dance, I am so focused on the Lord and ministry, that my skill level is quite reduced. In fact, I never do pirouettes on stage during a ministry dance. Instead, I may turn swiftly with both feet on the ground and legs straight (chenne turns in place) or I may simply walk quickly in a circle. I simply modify my movements so they may easily be accomplished. We want our focus to be on ministry and the message being presented, not the dancer's presentation of skill.

With this in mind, along with an understanding of body positioning, or "which is your better side," we can now go a little deeper with the discovery of the importance of various stage spaces.

Stage Placement

The stage space is not just one big area. It can be divided into several quadrants, each of which has varying significance from the other. With a basic understanding of these different areas and their worth, a dancer can take full advantage of its

Upstage Right	Upstage Center	Upstage Left
Center Stage Right	Center Stage	Center Stage Left
Downstage Right	Downstage Center	Downstage Left

capability. As you'll notice in the diagram, the stage can be divided into nine specific areas.

All these areas and their associated names refer to the dancer's right and left, not the audience's. In other words, if the dancer were to move 'stage right', they would move to their right (the audience's left). This is typical for actors as well as dancers. Upstage is labeled as such because back in ancient

Divine Choreography

Greek and Elizabethan theatre, the small stage spaces were raked upward slightly from the front to the back. The back of the stage lifted up (upstage) and the front of the stage angled slightly downward (downstage). They also used to recreate disproportionately sized furniture or props to compensate for the angle. This created an illusion of a deeper, larger room.

	UL	
	DL	

More specifically, there are certain areas that can be used for certain movements or ideas. Upstage left and downstage left, generally speaking, are rather weak areas on the stage. Stage left is also a weak position that may be good to use when you do not want to notice a dancer or dancers, during a time when other activity is going on at other places on the stage. It is a good place to put a dancer or dancers who have just finished their particular segment of the dance while the others are moving on to other things. It is also a good place to have the 'defeated foe' characters fall to their death.

UR		
DR		

Upstage right is somewhat stronger, even though there is distance from the audience. This distance creates curiosity and anticipation. This is a good place to start a dance or enter. Downstage right has a pretty good link with the audience and is good for shapes, poses, and body design to take place.

SR		

Stage right, on the other hand, is a wonderfully captivating location for a highlighted dancer to begin or move. Most people in the world, read from left to right. Therefore, stage right is a good area to put stronger or highlighted dancers. It is also a good place to begin a new movement phrase or do a featured portion of the dance. If you are in the audience, your eye will naturally tend to go toward that direction first and then travel to the right. Therefore, the audiences will easily and casually enjoy whatever is going on in that area. Also, there is a side note that may help your practice times or classes. When dancers on opposite sides of the stage, must cross each other, it is common to have the people on stage right cross in front of the people coming from stage left.

	CS	
	DC	

Although center stage is deemed as the strongest focal point, according to most people, there are those who believe that downstage center is the strongest. Movement in this area of the stage creates an intimacy with the audience and almost has an effect of coming out into the audience, which can evoke more of an emotional response. It creates greater impact with the audience. Many years ago, they used to create stages that actually jutted out into the audience to produce that same effect. I will almost always go out into the audience, leaving the stage space altogether. One word of caution, here: if you are going to do some of your dance on the floor (in between the pew and the stage) it is wise to avoid kneeling or doing movements on the floor, because the moment you go below waist level, from about the second or third row back, the audience will no longer be able to see you.

The upstage space, in and of itself, is typically weaker then its downstage counterparts. However, when used appropriately in a dance, it can add an intriguing charm to a character. If you've heard the phrase about someone "upstaging" another, it kind of sounds

	US	

like a 'pecking order' type of term (like "I'm better then you"). It seems rather a misnomer if this stage placement is supposed to be less valuable then downstage. However, in acting, a stage set may have two actors, both facing front (or at least slightly toward one another), and then one actor would begin walking backwards. For their conversation to continue, the backward walking action would force the stationary actor to turn his or her back toward the audience. Not only would the upstage character be more noticeable at that point, but also it would give that character more strength, hence making the downstage character appear weaker.

Nevertheless, any stage placement is conditional, based on relative positioning of other dancers and props on the stage. None of these are hard-fast rules to which one must strictly adhere. All the tips in this book are simply general guidelines and ideas from which you may draw to expand your thinking and understanding of how to present worship dance.

Value of Direction of Movement

The value of direction of movement is almost identical to the above-mentioned section. The addition of movement from one stage area to another marks the difference. I will discuss the variations of directional movement briefly, and then the charts will reiterate them visually.

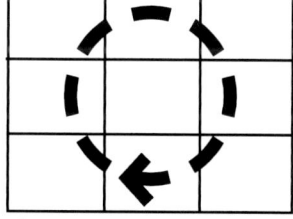

Circular—When this uplifting group movement is done on the stage space, it should pretty well be kept brief and used for variety within the dance. This type of dancing is typically used during feasts and celebrations as a festive, joyful expression. We see this round dancing in Hebrew folk dance. It is great to do during praise services where whole congregations are encouraged to join in and dance. This is the type of dancing that just begs for participation. What happens, sometimes, when a folk dance of this nature is used as a presentation piece (or part of one), is that the dancers have a wonderful time praising God, but often, the audience is left out as an observer, rather then a warmly invited participator.

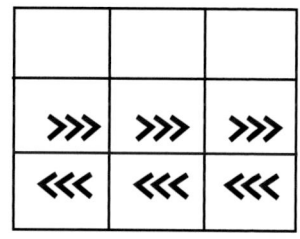

Side to Side—Similar to circular movements, side to side directional moving (when done repetitiously) becomes too flat and can be boring. It is, in and of itself, rather weak. The advantage here, though, is that if the dancers are facing front (as we mentioned earlier), their strength of body positioning may compensate for this anti-climatic direction. Again, like circular movements, however, if interjected intermittently with movements heading in other directions, it could be quite nice. So, it need not be thrown away altogether. In fact, it could become very interesting if the right body alignment and poses were used. Think about the direction you are going as well as the way you are facing.

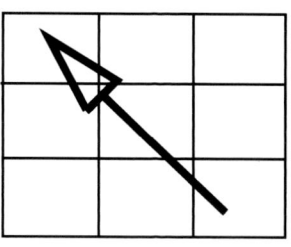

Downstage Left to Upstage Right—Although diagonal movement is typically viewed in drama as having a very sharp or direct quality, when it is done in this direction, it has almost the opposite effect. It is as if the actor is fading off into the distance. Think about a dramatic scene in a play where, perhaps a woman was to discover that her fiancé was dead. If she were moving toward him (upstage right), but away from the audience (downstage left), it would somehow loose its impact. This is considered a very weak direction in which to move.

Upstage Left to Downstage Right—Though still weak, in this direction the audience at least may feel like you are coming toward them. This would have slightly more impact than the one previously mentioned. The problem here is that most of the world reads from left to right and this kind of direction opposes that natural flow of observation. Remember, we are referring to the actor or dancer's right and left when we are talking about stage right and left. So, when we (or the audience) reads the movements from *their* left to right this can be subconsciously frustrating.

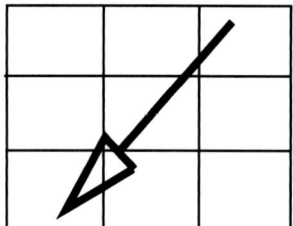

Downstage Right to Upstage Left—This may seem to contradict the statements about downstage left to upstage right, but it is a stronger directional choice. Even though it seems like the dancers are moving away from the audience or fading off into the distance, it can still be considered somewhat of a strong

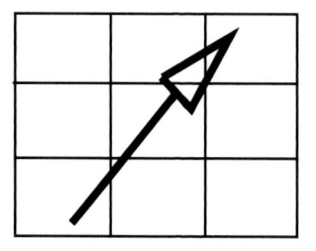

Divine Choreography

direction. This is only because of the 'reading rule' mentioned just above. Because the audience would be viewing with a more natural flow, their vista would be more pleasant and acceptable.

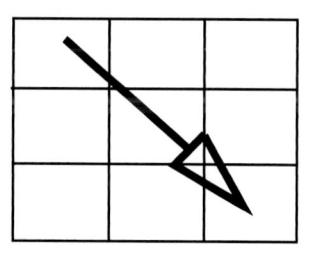

Upstage Right to Downstage Left—Because angles or diagonals have such a precise and absolute quality, they and especially this one should be reserved for very significant or climactic points in the dance. This point, by itself, gives this direction value. However, that in conjunction with the 'reading rule', gives it an extra boost to the top of the significance chart. When dancers move in this direction on a diagonal, the impact on the audience is quite strong. On the other hand, I will often *begin* dances upstage right and slowly work my way down to left only because it gives the movements a little more potency (particularly if it is a solo). It is also a good way to capture the audience's attention, like the attention-grabbing line in the opening of a good speech.

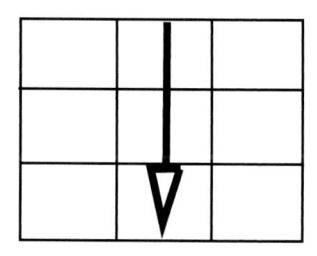

Upstage Center to Downstage Center—This is by far, the most passionate and powerful directional movement. It has almost a barrier breaking, emotionally intruding quality that creates intimacy with the audience. Once that barrier is broken, the impact becomes deeper and more heartfelt. It is quite intense, particularly if there are many dancers moving at a good speed right toward the audience and stopping just short of the edge of the stage (with a dramatic pose). It adds tremendous impact during a climactic highlight of the dance, again, captivating the audience and leaving them almost breathless.

Even though there are so many concepts to learn, some of them will be remembered when necessary. These are simply guidelines and suggestions. All these body directions, stage placements, and directions of movement ideas only scratch the surface to what can be done with them. There is a multitude of variables that can be associated with them. It depends on the music, the number of dancers, their relationship to one another on the stage space, and their skill level, Etc. So, be creative, as we serve a creative God. He *rejoices* over us. That word *rejoices* is *giyl* (in the Hebrew), which means to spin with a violent emotion of joy. If God Almighty Himself spins with intense emotion, how much more should we dance joyfully before Him, utilizing the passionate creativity that comes from Him?

Dance Development 5

Rhythm
Changes & Variation
Cannon

Rhythm

Now that we've come to a basic understanding of foundational concepts, we can move on to learn more specific ideas for dance development. It is essential to grasp the element of rhythm. This is something that can either leave your audience frustrated (when it is not used properly) or satisfied (when it is used to its maximum potential).

I'll never forget an exercise I was given, to prove a point about rhythm (in one of my choreography classes). My college professor had us do movement against some music. In other words, we had to not pay any attention to the beat, timing, or rhythm of the music. This had to have been one of the most difficult exercises I ever had to do. There had to be absolutely no rhythm. One girl tried to clean the mirrors in the studio for her assignment, thinking that it wasn't at all dance moves, but a simple household chore. On the contrary, the professor said that even her wiping of the mirror (with her arm moving up and down) contained rhythm. I really don't remember what I did, but I don't think it passed either. I think the only one who passed the exercise, was a young man who just sat on a stool and removed one of his contact lenses. There was absolutely no beat or rhythm to what he was doing. I suppose the point was that there is much rhythm in almost everything we do.

The point of this section is to reveal how to get the most out of this for effective presentations and dance development. There are a few specific types of rhythm that will be addressed.

When a song refers to or evokes a certain emotion, a dancer's response can create a certain type of rhythm. For example: if the song indicated that someone was sad or grieving, a typical response would be to contract in the midsection of the body and bend over. This could be repeated a number of times (with variation) and it would be rhythmic. This type of emotional rhythm usually evokes a response in the audience as well. They kind of 'feel your pain', which is part of the idea. It is good to involve the audience as much as possible in what you are doing or portraying. Variation, in the midst of emotional rhythm, makes it more convincing. An emotion of joy may be expressed through a rhythmic movement of skipping, followed by a lightweight run with the arms waving quickly overhead, from side to side. Now that you have been made aware of rhythm, can you see the variations in that one sentence alone? The skipping has kind of an 'offbeat' sound or feel, while a light run would probably be more regular in timing.

Our breathing has a natural rhythm of which we are not aware, most of the time. It becomes apparent when we are shocked and gasp for air or when we are frightened and begin to breath heavily. Of course, when we exercise after we have been out of shape for a while, our breathing becomes labored and heavy. We can use this natural form of rhythm as a guide to inhalation, suspension, and release (exhalation) as it transfers throughout the body. Suspension and release are wonderful rhythmic tools to use in a dance. It creates a moment of tension and a sigh of relief within the audience. For instance: Let's say a dancer was to run from upstage to downstage and then pause up on the balls of his or her feet, while indicating a longing look and a reaching of the arms (when arriving at the front of

Divine Choreography

the stage). This could then be followed by a 'release' type of move (or an emotional contraction could be interjected in the meantime) where the dancer would scoot backwards (like a balloon that lost its air).

In fact, it is kind of like inhaling, holding the breath for too long of a moment, and then gladly letting out the air. It is also kind of like a small boat, without an engine, being tossed to the crest of a wave and then sliding down into the trough; or it could be like climbing to the top of a roller coaster and then experiencing the release of going down after reaching the top. These scenarios can be quite suspenseful. People stand in line for a long time at the fairgrounds to experience that feeling. How much more could this type of rhythm be incorporated into our presentation pieces and also be effective?

Responding to gravity and the beat of the music has many more details and variations. Gravity plays a large part in our everyday lives and movements. If you were to hold your arm straight out to your side and then release it. The weight of your arm would immediately make it fall back to your side. There is a whole study in physics about gravity, speed, distance of an object's fall, Etc. However, for this discussion, we will focus specifically on the beat of music, our bodies' motor rhythm, and its energy's rising and falling in response to natural gravity.

There are patterns in time and rhythm in the movement (or movement phrases) and sections of the dance that make up those patterns. There is rhythmic shape and form (among other things). There are also types of forms within them. Let's start with an understanding of *rhythmic shape*. It is "the energy which starts the movement, keeps it going and stops it by application and release of force within its duration of time. The force punctuate (accents) and divide the time."[4] There can be the beginning accent, a middle accent or end accent. It is good to use all of them within a dance, to add interest.

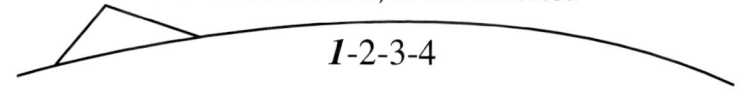

1-2-3-4

The beginning accent can be a fervent, quick accent that may begin the movement and then it may become slower and less powerful to finish in a disappearing or fading manner. So often, we get 'stuck' in this kind of timing or rhythm, where the accent is on count one. Perhaps it would be good to consider varying slightly.

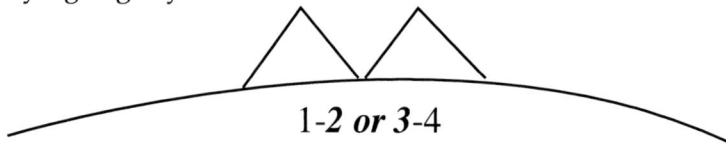

1-*2 or 3*-4

If a middle accent is used, it could build up and come in the middle of the movement or phrase. Let's say you wanted to do a hop on one leg with the other knee bent, with the toe up to the other knee. You could step on count one (bringing the knee up) and hop on two; or take two steps and hop on three. This would add more variety then to just hop or accent on count one. Perhaps you could do it one time on one and the next time on two or three. This keeps the dance from being predictable.

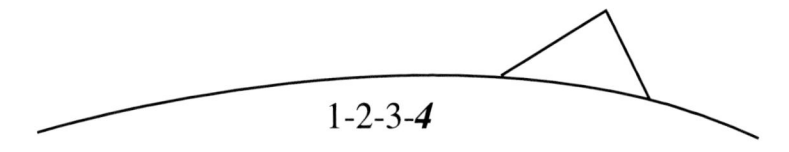

1-2-3-*4*

Finally, the end accent or end of the movement or movement phrase may become the most forceful, which would give a climax to the whole. These accents punctuate and divide the time to create a rhythmic shape.

A *rhythmic form* is the organization of that time and those accents or shapes into phrases and sections as they relate to movement. There are a few terms that I will point out here that may give more clarity to this concept.

A ──────────────────── B

Binary form (stemming from two) is like stitching section **A** with a contrasting section **B**, but sewing them together with a common thread or theme.

Divine Choreography

```
A───────────B───────────A
```

A ternary form, on the other hand, has an **A-B-A** sort of arrangement. Every now and then, it is good to let the audience be comfortable by letting them figure out what will come next, so they can have an "I knew that was going to happen" type feeling. This should be more the exception then the rule. The A sections can be almost identical with one another, making B a section of contrast. The A sections may be reversed from one another (like a mirror), or the elements may be the same but have their order changed around. Certain parts with in the A section may be highlighted, but they all must be closely associated with one another.

A-B	A-B-A	A-B-A	A-B
A-B	A-B-A	A-B-A	A-B

Now, rhythmic shape and form can be broken down into inner and outer form. The "inner form consists of the time, force (accent), or shape of each movement, movement phrase and section creates. Outer form consists of the shape brought about by the juxtaposition of each section in the dance, piecing it all together like an architect puts together the design elements of a house. Each part of the dance has relevance to the whole."[3] Basically, the inner form would be the types of movement done within sections **A-B-A** of the ternary form and the outer form would be the overall shape of the dance, which would be the ternary form itself. This is essentially just terminology for piecing together a dance so it all relates in some way or another. We want this in our presentation pieces, particularly in church, because to many people, dance is like a foreign language and it is the choreographer's responsibility to make the dance easy to understand so the message will minister.

Changes & Variation

During the development and construction of a dance, change and variation are essential and should be included to maintain interest. Lots of variety is the key in choreographed dances.

Lynn M. Hayden

The opposite is true for worship dance where there might be a group of people all doing the same thing at the same time. When you are leading praise and worship dancing, you need to totally ignore everything you learned and will have learned about variety and stick with simplicity, predictability, and repetition. Since this book is about choreographed presentation dances, we will continue with a look at the types of change that can be accomplished to spice the dance.

Going back to the elements of design, change can be a motif that should relate to the dance or have purpose (not just be there for change's sake alone). To dig a little more deeply, we will explore Laban's analysis of movement again with regard to change as the primary motif.

For an example of *quality* of movement change, a slow section of a movement, or movement phrase can be followed by a fast one. There can be a slow section of movements that all of a sudden contain fast (like double-time) movements. This would break up the continuity and add interest or pleasant surprise.

Different levels can be demonstrated on the stage space as well. The mere fact that dancers would be in different areas of the stage at the same time, adds depth of field or an illusion of levels.

Spatial changes could be going from small or low level movements and gradually moving to medium, and finally to high or large level movements. Of course, this can be reversed. This can be done as the movement of one or many dancers.

Level change, dramatic group poses, and sculpting are some of my favorite things to add to a dance. This visually adds so much depth and creativity to a portion of a dance that it should almost always be included. Examples of levels that can be used in a pose are: lying on the floor, sitting, kneeling on the feet, kneeling up, a long, low lunge, a comfortable lunge, and standing. The changes from standing or running to jumping or leaping also create even a higher level.

One example of an *action* change could be going from

Divine Choreography

stepping to jumping. Another one would be going from an expressive gesture to traveling. The emphasis of the action would be magnified if it were defined by stillness before or after the action.

Finally, *relationship* change has to do with the number of people added to or subtracted from the movement or movement phrase. This is rather obvious. If you were doing a nice group pose using all the different levels mentioned above, and wanted to incorporate a relationship change, three or four people could go elsewhere on the stage to create another formation while the remaining two recreate theirs. The relationship change occurs both when one group leaves and when new groups are formulated.

Variation and contrast offer so much to a dance. Though variation is very good, like change, itself, it too should have logical development or be viewed in different ways throughout the piece. The content of the dance should be used again several times in different ways with a logical understanding that emerges throughout the piece. Contrast, on the other hand, provides points of interest that stand out and add flavor to the dance, yet it relates to the theme. This can and often does become the highlight or climax of the dance.

I did a dance to "The Power of Your Love" that included both of these concepts. When the lyrics said "hold me close," I used the same kind of movement throughout the dance. However, for variation, I demonstrated it just a little bit differently each time. The first time, I had one person move forward and the rest of the dancers surrounded her in a semi-circle with their arms rounded over her (indicating a giant group hug). The second time, she moved forward and only one other dancer went behind her to give a hug indication. Finally, during the climax of the song, all the dancers put their arms out to the side and after what seemed like a suspension (or like a breath), they suddenly all hugged themselves. So, the same idea was repeated throughout the dance but it was done a little differently each time.

For contrast, within the same dance, I used different levels and arm movements. When the song said: "I'll rise up like the

Opposition & Contrast

eagles," I had the back line bend down with their arms out to their sides like a 'U' (elbows down and palms up), while the front line stood tall, with their arms out to their sides, with their elbows up and palms down. Every four counts, the lines would reverse their poses. This gave an up, down contrast, and looked like wings' movement. Oppositional and contrasting movements add so many new facets of height, width, breadth, depth, and length, that the dance automatically becomes more remarkable.

Cannon

In addition to rhythm, contrast, and variation, cannon is another wonderful element of design that makes a practical addition to your expanded vocabulary of choreography. This is not where you get shot across the sanctuary with large doses of gun powder, it is one part of the dance, movement, or movement phrase followed by another part in a time portion of the music. The time when one person or group goes in front of or behind another person or group (or where there are changes) can vary greatly.

Example 1: If the movement phrase is the same, one group may begin to move and the second group may come in momentarily after; or the first group may complete the phrase before the second group repeats it. The second, and subsequent groups may come in at any time after the first group. This sequence could be termed as *same movement cannon*. Once, I choreographed a dance to "All Honor" (Ron Kenoly) with one hundred and thirty people. There is a part in the song (toward the end) where the words "for fire" are repeated around eight times. Rather then doing the exact same thing all eight times, I had one row do a certain move for eight counts. Then, the second row joined them, so that two rows were then doing the same thing to the second count of eight. Likewise, the third row joined in during the third count of eight. There were other things that went on as well, but for the simplicity of this example's sake, I didn't want to describe all the other complicated details. You get the picture any way. By about the seventh count of eight, all one hundred and thirty people were expressing "for fire" in powerful unison. It was very intense!

Example 2: Another example of *same movement cannon* is when one or two people may start a sequence and then the second part of the phrase may include the rest of the group (or a large group); or a sequence may start with a large group, and be followed up with one or two people repeating the movements any time after the initial movement.

Example 3: The type of cannon that has a sequential effect is *continuous*. Movement that is done one right after the other (on the beat) is called single movement cannon. Following that by a phrase type cannon (group one then group two) could prove to be quite exceptional.

These next three examples are among my favorite. They really add a unique quality to a dance that kind of makes it stand out.

Example 4: *Complementary movement cannon* is like a question and answer. The dancer or dancers would make one type of movement or movement phrase (like a question), and it would then be followed by a harmonizing move (like an answer).

Example 5: *Contrasting movement cannon* is similar to complementary (with regard to timing). However, the design shapes within the movements vary and are done in a succession type style, such as: Up verses down; Soft verses hard; Sharp verses gentle; Round verses straight; Fast verses slow; Etc.

Example 6: Finally, one of my absolute favorites that can be used in praise and worship dancing as well as during presentation pieces is *background/foreground*. During this one, there could be a group or line of people in the back (upstage) for example, doing a very simple, repetitive movement while a soloist or smaller group of dancers does something a little more complicated in the foreground. Perhaps the background group could maintain the beat of the bass guitar or drums, while the

Background/Foreground

foreground person does movement to the melody or some higher pitched instruments. It has a very lovely effect.

Now that you have lots of choreography techniques derived from some of the basic elements of design, you should have many ideas with which to construct or develop your dance. Once the core of the dance is developed, it will be time to work on the ending of the composition, which is very important.

Fantastic Finale!
Ending & Exits
Presentation Protocol

Ending & Exits

Both the ending and then the exit of a dance are the vital ingredients to a fantastic finally and to the overall presentation. If there are many mistakes in the middle of the dance, the audiences will more then likely forgive and forget them if the ending is good, especially if they are left with a feeling of completion and satisfaction. The ending is the last thing the audience remembers and counts for almost one half of the dance's overall value. It should be true, but not predictable.

So often, in the past, I had worked so hard on the beginning and middle of the dance and then realized (a little too late) that I was quickly running out of time to practice the all-important ending. I learned to organize the rehearsal times more effectively so that there would be plenty of time to practice the ending repeatedly. Practicing the ending over and over again, until it feels almost like over learning, is good because then the dancers feel like they can worship and not worry. The dancers should not have to feel like they are concentrating so hard on the steps that their countenance becomes grimaced during the presentation. The ending will be crisp and leave a good taste in the audience's mouth, if it is well rehearsed.

Don't take a bow to the audience. Should the audience applaud, it is a good idea to indicate that the glory should go to the Lord. This doesn't have to be done in such a big showy way that it becomes like false humility. If you know that you did a good job, and you worked hard, it is all right to accept congratulations on a job well done, but be sure to give glory to the Lord from whom the inspiration came.

It is very important how you exit. This should be as nice and uniform as the entrance. If there are some dancers who end on their knees and some end standing, for instance, the ones standing should wait for the ones kneeling to stand, so they may all leave together. It is important to plan 'how' you will leave the stage space. Don't just kind of get up and walk off to your seat and another to the dressing room and another to the choir loft. Make some kind of formation: single file, or two by two, Etc. and go reverently down the aisle (or where ever it is you need to go to get out of sight). Maintain an attitude of worship all the way down the aisle. Once you are totally out of sight, you can share one another's excitement. If you do that too soon (or within earshot of the audience) it could also break the anointed flow. Try not to make contact with the audience during your exit (waving, giggling, hugging, Etc.). Until you are out of sight, you are still part of the team and the presentation.

Finally, it is also important to know 'when' to exit. It could make or break the feeling and flow of the whole piece. If the dance has a "ta-daaa" pose-type ending on the stage, it is good to hold that pose for a few seconds (before standing or getting into a formation). Once that pause in time has taken place, then everyone needs to slowly rise or turn or whatever they need to do in order to begin making an exit formation. What ever you do, don't linger longer. I did this once and learned my lesson well. We did a dance that had about sixty people. It was at a conference again, where the participants participated. We did the whole dance and ending successfully (with the music's completion), on the stage. The people applauded vigorously. We appropriately gave the glory to the Lord, but it wasn't until the applauding began to subside, when we realized that we needed to get off the stage (so the conference hosts could move on to other things). Because there were so many people, it took a very long time to exit. By the time the last dancer was out of sight, the audience was *really* ready to move on to other things.

What I have discovered, more recently, that works exceptionally well, is to incorporate the exit into the ending of the song. Some songs kind of fade out at the end anyway. Why not fade off stage with the music? Then by the time that the last note is heard, the last dancer is out of sight. The stage becomes clear and the service can move on to whatever is next. If there are a large number of dancers that have to exit, have some begin leaving before the music actually fades. Later, have subsequent dancers follow suit.

I always like to minister to the audience somehow during the song and if it is not done in the middle, I have the dancers make some kind of motion (like throwing blessings from their cupped hands, for instance) toward the audience while they are exiting. Of course, whatever gesture you do toward the audience would have to correspond with the song.

Some songs have a very strong, almost explosive ending. During this type of song, it may be good to have a brief "ta-daaa" (or pose) ending and then have everyone briskly run out in formation, while the music is reverberating its last sounds. Remember, endings and exits are vital, so practice, practice, practice for a fantastic finale!

Presentation Protocol

There are several 'unspoken rules' that apply to presentation dances. These are the kinds of things that are like a diplomatic agreement that amend and clarify some ideas about dance in the church. They are rather scattered with regard to subject and order, but are simply helpful tips learned from observation and personal experience. Many of these ideas and suggestions are in appendix A in a more encapsulated form.

One note of presentation protocol worth mentioning, is that if you are scheduled to present during a certain time in the service, be sure to be ready. For example, if you are supposed to present your dance immediately following the offering, be sure that you are in place and ready to go, so the congregation doesn't have to wait. If there is an announcement for your dance, there is nothing worse then to have them announce: "and now, the dance team will present....," but no one is in place. They announce for the second time: "the dance team will now present...," and only a few people are ready, but no one can progress until everyone is there. The leadership has to make a call at that moment, (which puts them in a very awkward position) whether to move on to something else or make the congregation wait until everyone is ready.

Be sure that if you are scheduled to go on right after offering, that you line up and be ready *during* offering. They shouldn't even have to make an announcement. The whole team should be ready to immediately get into starting positions. Usually, Sunday morning is a time where so much must be covered: Praise & worship, announcements, baby dedications, possibly communion, music or dance specials, oh yeah and the Pastor may want to give a sermon and maybe even an alter call! There is a tinge of pressure on leadership to be able to please all the department heads and squeeze everything into an hour or two. It would be nice to forgo all the agendas and focus on spending time in God's presence, but there are times when everything just has to fit. Therefore, if your dance is on the agenda, during your scheduled time frame, carry the responsibility of prompt and smooth service transition.

Secondly, a few related things I see quite often and should mention are singing, gum chewing, and fidgeting before and during presentation pieces. There is no hard and fast rule written in cement about the subject, but take the information for what it is worth and apply it where necessary. We learned earlier that the audience's eye is drawn to that which is moving the most. So, if you are in a group of dancers and are the only one singing or even chewing gum, guess to where the audience's eye will be attracted? The chomping motion (while chewing gum) or lip and jaw moving motion (while singing) could be a distraction to the overall message of the song. This same idea holds true for fidgeting on stage, before the music begins. Be sure your costume is situated before you go on and that you are comfortable. Be

Divine Choreography

sure to have an extra measure of patience and stillness while you are waiting for the music to begin. Remember, all eyes are on you.

Finally, if you make a mistake during the dance, don't let your face or actions show it. Most of the time, the audience will never know the difference anyway. If you are doing a solo, and mess up, they will definitely not notice, because no one knows the choreography accept you. If it is a small group of dancers and you forget something or go the wrong way, chances are that the audience will just assume that the choreographer added some out of the ordinary nuance. If you are in a large group and experience mishap, more then likely, the audience won't even notice it, because they are watching the presentation as a whole. If they do notice, they may think that it is very interesting choreography.

One time I saw a dance that had quite a few dancers (maybe thirty). Everything was going along fine until this one dancer made a mistake. The only reason that I noticed it was that she made that 'rolling of the eyes' look of exasperation. That was somewhat noticeable. Then she made another mistake, but this time she stopped her movement and expressed her frustration with hand signals. This time, more then likely, the whole audience empathized with her.

I've got to tell on myself. I've been teaching this concept about never letting your face show it and keeping the dance going as if nothing ever happened, for years. This one particular concert (to make a long story short), I put on different ballet shoes then I had been wearing all day and thought I heard a still small voice say: "those shoes are slippery." After promptly ignoring the warning, you can only imagine what happened. Very shortly after the dance began, BOOM! Flat on my behind I fell. Well instead of doing what I had been teaching all these years, I simply sat there, looked at the audience and blurted out: "can you believe I did that?!" Some people wanted me to keep going, but I deliberately got up, asked them to play the music over and I just did it again, with no spills. I don't recommend that you do this, but I just wanted to share a true story.

Later on in that week, I had a chance to redeem my blunder. I was doing a rather spontaneous dance and saw a lovely piece of red material that would go 'oh so appropriately' with the song. I proceeded to gracefully whisk by, and scoop up the long cloth. All of a sudden, it got stuck! Well, after all, I was the teacher and wasn't going to let my face show it this time. So, I turned my back to the audience, pretended to turn it into a representation of the blood of Jesus, while I made a pose of a cross. I was able to observe where it was stuck and backtrack to that point while maintaining a cross pose. I then released it and moved on. There was certainly a bit of momentary tension, but it all worked out and the dance ministered.

Those things seen as proper and correct to help your dance's overall acceptance are considered presentation protocol. If these, in conjunction with the tips in appendix A are utilized, your dances should be well received and presented successfully. These, good entrances and exits, along with other do's and don'ts, help to not only give a fantastic overall presentation, but also put the finishing touches on a fantastic finale!

Conclusion

From beginning to end, entrance to exit, and everything in between, there is a communication form of Spirit design. Whether you use one or all of the choreography techniques is not as important as bringing into existence and creating something new from a divine inspiration. It is not important that you remember all the techniques. The important thing is that an audience remembers (or is impressed by) the Holy Spirit's divine inspirational design, demonstrated through anointed human vessels. However, the accomplishment of this goal can be obtained more succinctly and deliberately through good choreography technique. Therefore, the combination of divine inspirations and choreography technique can turn an ordinary dance into *divine choreography*. The result is not only an emotional touch, for those with whom the dance comes in contact, but ministry...

Appendix

Basic Do's & Don'ts

This appendix is designed as a brief summary and reiteration of some of the topics that were discussed previously. Some of them are entirely new and helpful hints. Also, many of these are found in the Dancing For Him book, which I highly recommend to every minister of dance. They are an encapsulated version of what type of presentation and choreography mistakes to avoid and tips for which to adhere.

- ***Don't*** Just walk on stage haphazardly (cutting up and not standing in ready position).
- ***Do*** Enter in an orderly, reverent manner. Be well rehearsed.
- ***Don't*** Make people wait a long time while you get to the platform.
- ***Do*** Be ready to go, so service runs smoothly.
- ***Don't*** Show impatience with the soundman (rolling of the eyes, using hand motions to move him along more quickly, Etc.).
- ***Do*** Have patience with the sound person. While waiting for music to begin, hold your position.
- ***Don't*** Have a sloppy appearance.
- ***Do*** Have a nice neat appearance with uniformity in dress. Everyone in the dance should have either ballet shoes or bare feet (not some in shoes and some, not). Bare feet are

best with pants or a modern type dress; however, they are not recommended with a worship dress or skirt.
- ***Don't*** Adjust costume, fix hair, or rub eyes, especially while you are waiting in place for the music to begin, as the congregation's eyes head straight for your movement (however small and insignificant it may seem).
- ***Do*** Make sure your costume is situated before you go on. If a part of the costume should fall off, make the best of it as if it never happened, and the congregation will soon forget there was a problem.
- ***Don't*** Chew gum!! It's distracting and hazardous to your health (should you jump and choke on it).
- ***Do*** Smile from your heart.
- ***Don't*** Sing when doing a presentation dance. The congregation will look directly at the person who is singing and may miss the message of the dance.
- ***Do*** Know the song and sing it in your heart.
- ***Don't*** Be immodest (with no leotard under your overlay or tunic; no culottes, Etc.)
- ***Do*** Pay careful attention to complete modesty, as we want to bring glory to God and bring the congregation's focused attention to Him.
- ***Don't*** Look at the feet of the person in front of you or at your fellow dancers for spacing, advice, direction, or cueing (unless your are doing improvisation).
- ***Do*** Keep your eyes focused on the Lord. Know the dance.
- ***Don't*** Goof and let your face show it, or fix your mistakes in the middle of them. Generally, the congregation will never know you made a mistake unless you tell them with your expression of dismay or by obvious corrections.
- ***Do*** Keep moving and smiling as if nothing had happened.
- ***Don't*** Do small inward type movements on stage, as they get lost in a large auditorium.
- ***Do*** Make your movements larger then life, so they can be appreciated by the back row as well as the front.
- ***Don't*** Do a solo with more then one person. In other

Divine Choreography

words, having two or more people doing all the same movements all at the same time, all the same way, in the same direction. That is boring.
- *Do* Vary your movements. Have some similar movements throughout the dance, but perhaps change the level (kneel, lunge or stand) on which you do them. As the chorus repeats, repeat the movement but perhaps add a variation on the same theme (movements get larger as the music gets stronger).
- *Don't* Do something that you cannot execute well.
- *Do* Movements that are your skill level or below. Otherwise, the lack of skill in that area will become a distraction.
- *Don't* Give them the whole picture in the beginning.
- *Do* Start with simplicity and build complexity as the dance progresses.
- *Don't* Have a sloppy ending. The ending's value is about almost fifty percent of the dance. The audience wants emotional satisfaction.
- *Do* Practice the ending of the dance. It is very important because it is the last thing the congregation remembers! Be sure to work on it extensively as the viewers may forgive and forget mistakes in the beginning and middle if the ending is good. It should be true, but not predictable.
- *Don't* Bow to the audience and take all the credit. Never take the glory to yourself.
- *Do* Direct all the glory to the Lord when and if people clap.
- *Don't* Exit by: just walking off and talking to each other; finding your seat; or maybe waving to someone in the congregation, Etc. It's a good idea to exit while they are still clapping, as it is rather anticlimactic to exit while the church is ready to move on to other things and they're just waiting for you to get out of the way.
- *Do* Plan your exit. Have uniformity and order. Maintain an attitude of worship until you are out of sight.
- *Don't* Do a duet while facing front the whole time. It becomes too flat and boring.
- *Do* Use some asymmetrical movements and poses as well as other variety.

Appendix B

Creative Activations

Activation simply means to learn by doing. This appendix is designed to help you with some practical applications for the techniques you just learned. They are a few of the actual exercises that I had previous workshop participants do. The following are from my notes and they are, therefore, somewhat cryptic. The idea is to help you with exercises that you may want to incorporate into your dance team practice times, or you may want to teach a workshop, yourself. Hopefully, this will stimulate your thinking so you may come up with your own exercises. Not only do these exercises help you with the concepts, but also they should help the creative thinking processes when you incorporate the new terminology and concepts into your choreography.

Dance Composition
Movement and Meaning

Purpose: To stimulate creative thinking. To discover the many variations of movement and movement phrases that can be done in choreographed (as well as spontaneous) dances. To reveal the depth and breadth of physical movement possibilities that will enhance and activate the worshipper's vocabulary of expression. Therefore, the learned, quality variations planted with in the worship dancer, will give greater meaning to their outward demonstration of gospel presentations.

Exercise 1: Basic Variations

Take the following action phrases and combine them with the following quality variations (4 counts of 8).

TRAVEL — TURN — OPEN — CLOSE

With large or small movements
With varying levels (high, medium and low)
With varying directions
With varying pathways on the floor

Exercise 2: Expanded Variations

Take the following action phrases and combine them with the following quality variations (4 counts of 8).

"TRAVEL — TURN — OPEN — CLOSE

With time emphasis
Quickly or slowly
Accelerating or Decelerating
With weight emphasis
Strongly or lightly
Increasing or decreasing degrees of tension
With flow emphasis
Bound stoppable and stopping or Continuous and free"[3]
Composition Concert Assignment
Combine one Basic Variation with one Expanded Variation to create a short (1 minute) dance. No music.

Exercise 3: Phrase Types

Use each of the following individual words or phrases to express a different idea (4 counts of 8).

"Action Phrases:
Set 1:

Rise	Fall
Travel	Open
Close	

Divine Choreography

Set 2:

   Gesture leading into a turn
   Travel into balance
   Tip into transference of weight
   Stretch and rise
   Travel and leap

Quality Phrases:
Set 1:

   From firm tension, gradually lose tension to become light
   Move quickly and lightly
   Relax three parts of body successively
   Become firm
   Release all tension and collapse

Set 2:

   Move with free flow
   Move with bound flow
   Make a series of bound and sudden movements
   Travel quickly, and with free flow to end in sudden and firm stillness

Set 3:

   Move lightly and slowly
   Move slowly with changing tensions
   Move quickly alternating between firm and light qualities
   Spin accelerating and decelerating to end in a firm body shape

Spatial Phrases:
Set 1:

   Move with a constantly changing focus
   Move with a fixed focus
   Change focus and then move… repeat this three times
   Focus on one body part and move into different directions
   Focus high and then low

Set 2:

> Start with very small movements and increase in size to very large
> Move with very large movements
> Alternately move one side of the body with small gestures and the other side with large gestures
> Intersperse large and small movements
> Make or finish with one movement, which gradually expands from small shape to a large shape, or, reverse."[3]

Composition Concert Assignment

Choose any set and create a short (1 Minute) dance using the whole set phrase.

Values of Direction of Movement

1. Upstage Center to Down Stage Center
2. Upstage Right to Down Stage Left
3. Down Stage Right to Upstage Left
4. Upstage Left to Down Stage Right
5. Down Stage Left to Upstage Right
6. Then Side-to-Side movement where R to L is better then L to R.
7. Circular Movements

EXERCISE:

Divide into 7 groups. Each group creates 8 counts of movement traveling in the appropriate direction. Use slow worship music, then strong music with a distinctive beat.

Dance Construction
Using CHANGE as the Primary Motif

Change – Normally, change should relate to the dance – have a purpose (not just for the sake of changing) Ex.- "Power of Love" – All change from DSL >>DSR to comfort Wendy

Divine Choreography

Types of Change

Quality "Slow section or movements – followed by fast Slow section containing fast movements to break continuity

Spatial Small, low level to large, high level movement Change of focus in space

Action Stepping to jumping Emphasis on an action, defined by stillness before or after the action

Relationship +/- # of people moving - Contrast in group"[3]

EXERCISE:
   Divide into 8 groups. Each group takes 5 minutes to create 8 counts of movement that is using a CHANGE category

Groups:
   1 & 2 Use – *Quality*
   3 & 4 Use – *Spatial*
   5 & 6 Use – *Action*
   7 & 8 Use - *Relationship*

Elements of Design Using Copy, Compliment, and Contrast

EXERCISES:
   Copy: Get a partner. One copies the pose of the other exactly. One person makes a shape while the other person makes a replica. Two poses each.
Do one pose of each: Copy, Contrast, & Compliment

Contrast: 2 groups of about 4 people each.

   Group 1 flows from stage R>>>stage L in 2 counts of 8 in a rounded, melodic, harmonious relationship.
   Curved body shapes
   Curved pathways on the floor
   Curved movements in the air
   Group 2 flows from stage L>>>stage R in 2 counts of 8 in a regimented and disciplined relationship.
   Straight, angular body shapes
   Move in straight-line pathways on the floor
   Straight movements in the air
   Groups switch

Compliment: Same groups of 4 – Each group make 4 separate group poses (with a different person leading each time).
Combine Copy, Compliment and Contrast to create a dance

Copy: 2 People create movements to: "Jesus, lover of my soul – Jesus, I will never let you go" – make exact copy of one another (no levels or compliments). Or this could be 2 parts with 2 people each.

Contrast: 2 people create contrasting movements to: "You've taken me from the miry clay – set my feet upon the Rock and now I know" – Or this could be 2 parts with 2 people each.

Compliment: 4 groups of 2 people each or 1 large group of 4 making 4 different poses or movements: "I love you, I need you. Though my world may fall, I'll never let you go."

Combination of A, B, & C
  Group A - create a copy movement to: "My Savior"
  Group B - create a contrast movement to: "My closest friend
  Group C - create a compliment movement to: "I will worship you until the very end:
  All repeat until the end of song.

Rhythm
Beginning Accent
Middle Accent
End Accent

EXERCISE:
  Groups of 4 – Create 4 counts of movement moving from stage L > stage R: All do the same thing. Do 3 different ways (changing the accent each time).

Rhythmic Form

Binary Form: Section A contrasted by section B with a common thread that binds them together.

EXERCISE:
  Divide your group in ½. Group A do 4 counts of movement then wait while Group B does contrasting movement. They each must have a thread of similarity, which binds one to the other like brother and sister.

Divine Choreography

Ternary Form: A-B-A arrangement.

EXERCISE:

Divide your group of 4 in ½ (2 in group A – 2 in group B). A do 4 counts of movement. Then B do 4 counts of contrasting movement. Then A do 4 more counts of movement that was very similar to their 1st 4 counts.

Shape and Form
Inner Form & Outer Form

Example: Inner form would be the types of movement done *within* sections A, B, A of the Ternary form and Outer form would be the overall shape of the dance—The Ternary form itself.

EXERCISE:

Get into 8 groups. Divide up Psalm 29:2-5 into 8 sections. Each group gets a scripture. Form a large semi-circle from L>R (1-8).

Inner Form: Each group creates movement (in the same 4 counts) to the scripture making the rhythmic dynamics similar to how the words sound. Ex.- *The Lord is over many waters* sounds like 1&2&3&4 (kind of a light and quick quality). *Worship the Lord in the beauty of holiness* sounds even like: 1,2,3,4 (kind of slow, and soft quality). Be careful not to do even beats. When it comes time to interpret your verse, your group says it out loud.

Outer Form: Piecing it together with a common thread (the overall formation of the dance). Everyone walks forward,2,3,4 and backward,2,3,4. At the same time everybody claps,2,3,4, continuously. Everyone continues to do this throughout the whole piece except when it is your turn to interpret your scripture verse. At the end, everyone says and does simple movements to: "And in His temple everyone says GLORY!" "The Lord will bless His people with peace."

SCRIPTURE

1. Give unto the Lord the glory due to His name (even then quick)

2. Worship the Lord in the beauty of holiness (slow and even)

3. The voice of the Lord is over the waters (calm > surprise on over)

4. The God of glory thunders (strong 3 accents)

5. The Lord is over many waters (varied—up & down)

6. The voice of the Lord is powerful (strong ending)

7. The voice of the Lord is full of majesty (strong beginning)

8. The voice of the Lord breaks the cedars (strong ¾)

Index

KEY WORD	PAGE
Action Phrase	33
Alignment	42
Binary form	54
Body positioning	42
Cannon	58
Changes	55
Choreography	7
Complimentary	38
Contrasting	39
Copy	38
Divine	7
Ending	61
Exits	61
Grand Entrances	25
Inner form	55
Inspiration	7
introductions	25
Laban's Analysis Movement	30
Level change	56
Motif	29
Outer form	55
Placement	44
Presentation protocol	63
Rhythm	51
Solo	22
Symmetry	35
Technique	7
Ternary Form	55
Value of Direction of Movement	47
Variation	55

Bibliography

[1] *The Exhaustive Concordance of the Bible*
Abingdon Press, Nashville Forty-second Printing 1983
James Strong Madison, N.J.
Key Word Comparison © 1980 by Abingdon

[2] *Spirit Filled Life Bible – New King James Version*
Scripture quotations and some comments
Thomas Nelson Publishers – Nashville – Atlanta – London – Vancouver
Thomas Nelson, Inc. ©1991

[3] *Dance Composition*
Jacqueline M. Smith-Autard
A&C Black (Publishers) Limited
35 Bedford Row, London WC1R 4JH
©1992 Originally published 1976 by Lepus Books ©1976

[4] *Webster's New World Dictionary of the American Language*
 Simon and Schuster, a division of Gulf and Western Corp. ©1982
1230 Avenue of the Americas
New York, New York 10020

Mission Statement

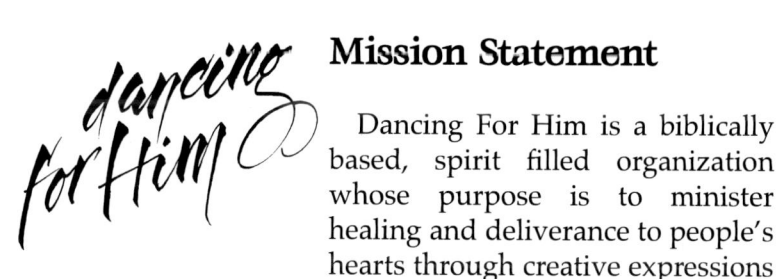

Dancing For Him is a biblically based, spirit filled organization whose purpose is to minister healing and deliverance to people's hearts through creative expressions of worship, prophesy, and dance. As artistic ministers who transcribe the heart of God into an acceptable life changing form, we exist to teach others about this unique art form through which to spread the gospel of Jesus Christ and set captives free!

Dancing For Him Worship Dance conferences are only phase I of a Five-Phase plan. This is to: minister, train, and activate others to effectively reach the lost; heal the sick, wounded and broken hearted; and open prison doors to those who are bound. During these awe-inspiring conferences, technical dance training is obtained; but more important, an impartation of anointing to minister through music and dance is transmitted. Please visit our website to see the other phases.

Lynn M. Hayden

For Further Information About:

Attending one of our conferences
Hosting a workshop in your area
Getting on our mailing list

Please feel free to contact us at:

Dancing for Him Ministries, Inc.
(800) 787-1623
info@dancingforhim.com
www.dancingforhim.com